# THE AMAZING HONEY BEE

## LEVEL  READER

READING LEVEL
2
GRADES 1 TO 3

Contributing writer: Susan Ring
Illustrations by Kim and James Neale

Copyright ©2011 Dalmatian Press, LLC. All rights reserved.
Printed in Guangzhou, Guangdong, China.

Franklin, Tennessee 37068-2068. 1-866-418-2572.
No part of this book may be reproduced or copied in any form without written permission
from the copyright owner. CE14255/0711

# Friends of the Earth

Do you like blueberries, apples, almonds, and carrots? Then, thank little honey bees! Honey bees visit the flowers of these plants, looking for sweet nectar. The dusty pollen of the flowers sticks to the bees' legs and gets passed from flower to flower. This is called *pollination*. This pollen-sharing helps plants make *new* plants—and more yummy fruits!

Honey bees also visit cotton plants, and the clover and grasses eaten by cows and sheep. So we can thank honey bees for milk, warm wool, and cool cotton!

**The Buzz**
Honey bees carry pollen back to the hive in "pollen baskets" on their back legs.

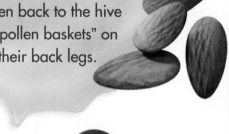

**The Buzz**
What makes the buzzing sound? It's the bee's wings flapping almost 200 times a second!

# Wings and Stings

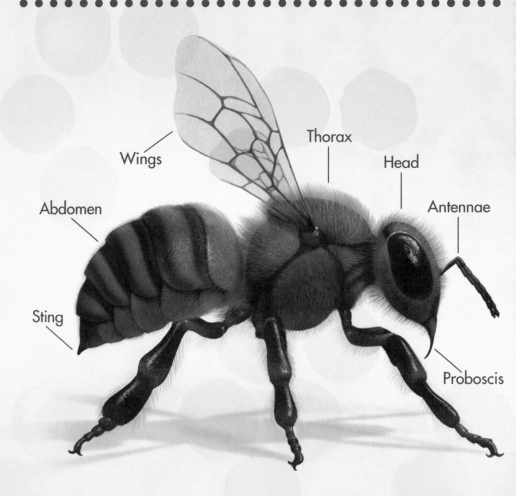

Wings

Thorax

Head

Antennae

Abdomen

Sting

Proboscis

Honey bees are insects, like butterflies, ants, and beetles. They have three main body parts and six legs. Honey bees also have wings—and a sting! A bee will only use her sting if she or the hive is in danger from a pest—like a careless human! For most people, a bee sting is painful but not harmful. But for the bee, using (and losing) her sting also means losing her life.

# Honey Bee Cousins

Bumble bees may also buzz about your garden, pollinating flowers. These big, furry bees eat pollen and nectar, just like honey bees. They also make a little honey, but they don't store it. They build small nests that only last a few months.

Bumble Bee

Wasps, hornets, and yellow jackets look like bees, but these fellows are not as friendly. If an animal (or person) gets close, they will attack as a group.

Yellow Jacket

And these insects do not lose their sting. They can jab again and again! Ouch!

Hornet

**The Buzz**
Bees collect sticky sap from trees and use it to glue and repair the sides of the hive.

# Master Builders

Wild honey bees make their hives in hollow logs, holes in trees, or under rocks. Worker bees remove flakes of wax from their bodies. They use this beeswax to build *chambers* (rooms) filled with combs, which are walls with *cells* (cuplike holes). All the cells have six sides that fit together perfectly to form the combs. The cells are used to hold eggs, pollen, and . . .

**The Buzz**
Beeswax has been used to make candles, shoe polish, and lipstick.

# Nature's Perfect Food

. . . HONEY!

A honey bee sips plant nectar through a *proboscis* (long mouth-tube). She takes nectar to the hive and places it into a cell in a comb. Many worker bees fan these filled cells with their wings. This turns it into thick honey!

**The Buzz**
During the summer months, honey bees store honey inside the hive to eat when winter arrives.

# Like Sweet Sunshine!

Honey bees are the only insects that make food that people eat. Bees store their honey in the cells of a honeycomb. Each cell is capped with wax, so the honey can be eaten later— by the bees or by us! Yum!

# From Egg to Bee

Honey bees are *social* insects. This means they live and work together as one large group, called a *colony*. Each colony has one queen. She has a big job. She lays eggs—lots of them!

The queen places a tiny egg in each cell of a brood comb. The egg hatches into a little white *larva* (plural: *larvae*). Nurse bees tend the larvae, cleaning and feeding them. For three days they feed them a soft food called royal jelly. Then they feed them nectar, honey, and bee bread (a mix of pollen and honey).

Here is a tiny egg that the queen has laid. Can you find more eggs?

The larvae then begin to change. They spin soft hairs around themselves into a cocoon. They now don't need to eat, so nurse bees cap their cells with wax. Inside a cocoon a young bee changes into a *pupa* (plural: *pupae*), and then into an adult bee. Adult bees hatch from the cells, ready to join the colony as worker bees.

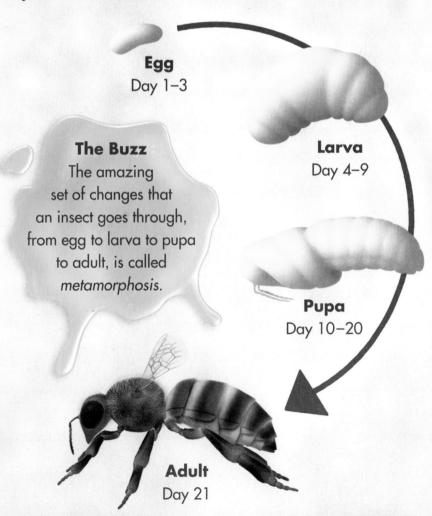

**Egg**
Day 1–3

**The Buzz**
The amazing set of changes that an insect goes through, from egg to larva to pupa to adult, is called *metamorphosis*.

**Larva**
Day 4–9

**Pupa**
Day 10–20

**Adult**
Day 21

# Lots of Sisters!

A honey bee colony can be huge, often having 60,000 bees. Almost all are female worker bees, born from eggs laid by one queen—so they are all sisters.

Queen

Worker

Drone

# Queen

Each colony has one queen. When she is a larva she is fed only royal jelly. This helps her grow large. She lives for 2 to 3 years and can lay 1,000 to 2,000 eggs a day!

# Workers

Worker bees are very busy sisters! They collect nectar and pollen, make wax, build, clean and guard the hive, make and store honey, and feed the queen and larvae. They also keep the hive cool by fanning their wings.

# Drones

Each colony has about 100 male bees, called drones. They only have one job—to mate with the queen bee. They do this just once, and then they leave the hive.

# The Waggle Dance

Perhaps the most amazing thing about honey bees is that they "talk" to each other through a special dance. If a bee finds a good nectar or pollen spot, she returns to the hive to tell the others. She walks in a figure-eight path and waggles as she moves through the middle of the path.

It's dark in the hive, so the bee gives off a smell that says, "Gather around and feel my dance! I have some news!" If she is very excited about her find, she will dance faster and stronger.

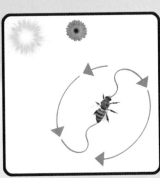
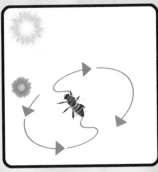

| This says "Fly toward the sun." | "Fly to the right of the sun, far off." | "Fly to the left of the sun, close by." |

In the waggle dance, if the bee waggles straight up toward the top of the hive, this means fly toward the sun. The direction of the waggle line tells the others which way to go.

The length of the waggle tells how far away the flowers are. The longer the waggle, the farther away the good nectar spot. When the flowers are close by, the waggle is short.

# Beekeeping

People have been harvesting honey and beeswax for thousands of years. Beekeepers "tame" colonies of bees by making cozy box hives for them to live in, year after year.

Many beekeepers lend their bees out to farmers. The bees fly around the farmland or orchard and pollinate the crops. When they are done, they return to the hive—ready to be moved to the next farm.

A beekeeper's wooden box hives have "rooms" with frames that are easy to slip in and out. There is space between frames, so bees can move easily about. The bees build combs in the frames, using one room for eggs and one for honey.

A beekeeper uses smoke to calm the bees. Then he can safely remove frames to harvest honey.

# Swarming

What happens when a hive gets too crowded? It's time to go house hunting. This often happens in late spring. Worker bees eat their fill of honey and then spend their time looking for a new place to build a hive. Once they find a good spot, they return and do a waggle-dance to tell others where it is.

About half the workers and the queen form a *swarm* (large group) and move to this new spot. A few days later, a new adult queen hatches in the old hive and begins to lay eggs.

When swarming takes place, the queen will start laying eggs in queen cups, so there will be a queen to replace her when she leaves.

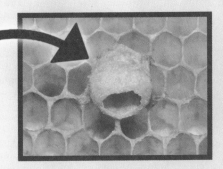

# Honey Bee Alert!

Life is not always easy for honey bees. They can get eaten by birds and other animals. Honey bees can also get sick. A few years ago, people reported that many colonies were dying. Honey bees flew out to collect nectar and pollen, but did not return. The whole colony would then *collapse* (become weak or die).

Scientists think that small bugs, stress, or a virus may be causing honey bees to die off at a faster rate than in the past. Many people are working very hard to solve this mystery and help save the honey bees. Without honey bees, many plants do not get pollinated.

# Be a Bee Pleaser

You can help! Plant a honey bee garden to attract honey bees. It's fun to watch honey bees visit flowers—but don't get too close! The bees have important work to do. If you startle a bee, it might sting you.

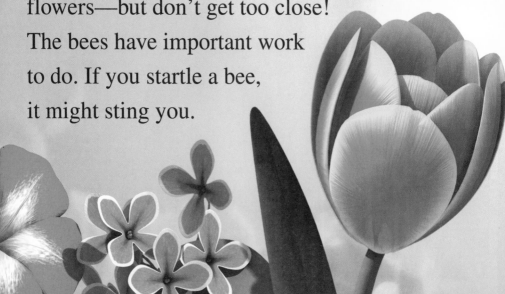

There are so many flowers that bees love. Here are just a few: Rose, sunflower, tulip, daisy, petunia, lilac, daffodil and clover.

**The Buzz**
Honey bees can fly 10 to 15 mph and will visit up to 100 flowers in one trip!

# Thank You, Honey Bees

We all need honey bees! These amazing workers spread pollen, which helps plants make fruits and seeds. And they make yummy honey—one of Nature's perfect foods!

So the next time you eat honey or see a bee sipping nectar, or hear it buzz as it finds a blossom, say, "Thank you, honey bees!"